Lewis Trondheim

Mister O

NANTIER · BEALL · MINOUSTCHINE
Publishing inc.
new york

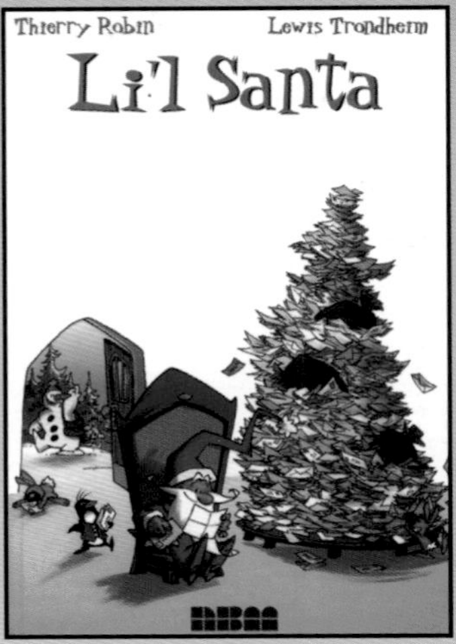
Thierry Robin
Lewis Trondheim
Li'l Santa

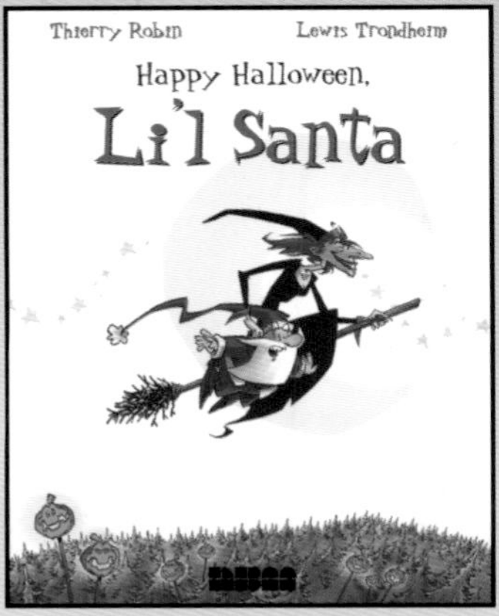
Thierry Robin
Lewis Trondheim
Happy Halloween,
Li'l Santa

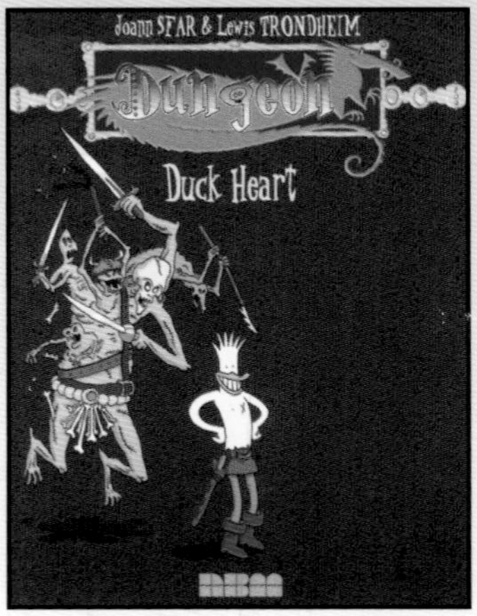
Joann SFAR & Lewis TRONDHEIM
Dungeon
Duck Heart

ISBN 1-56163-382-8

2nd printing
Printed in Singapore

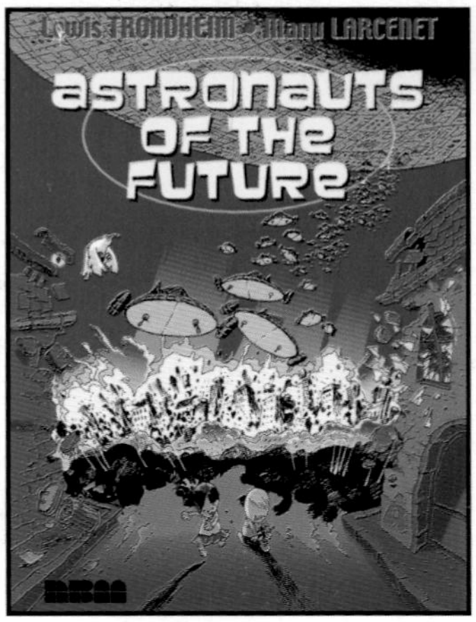
Lewis TRONDHEIM
Manu LARCENET
ASTRONAUTS OF THE FUTURE

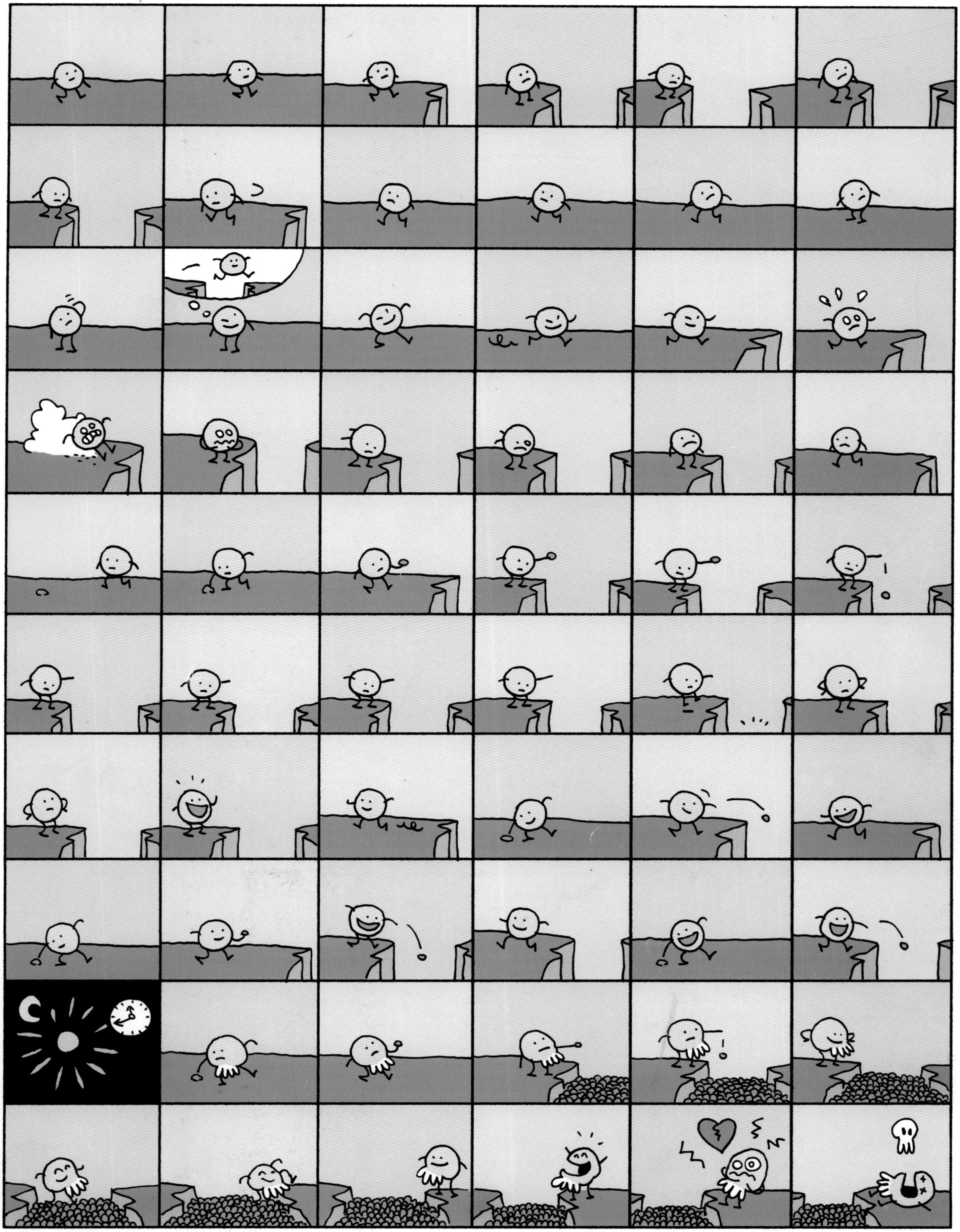

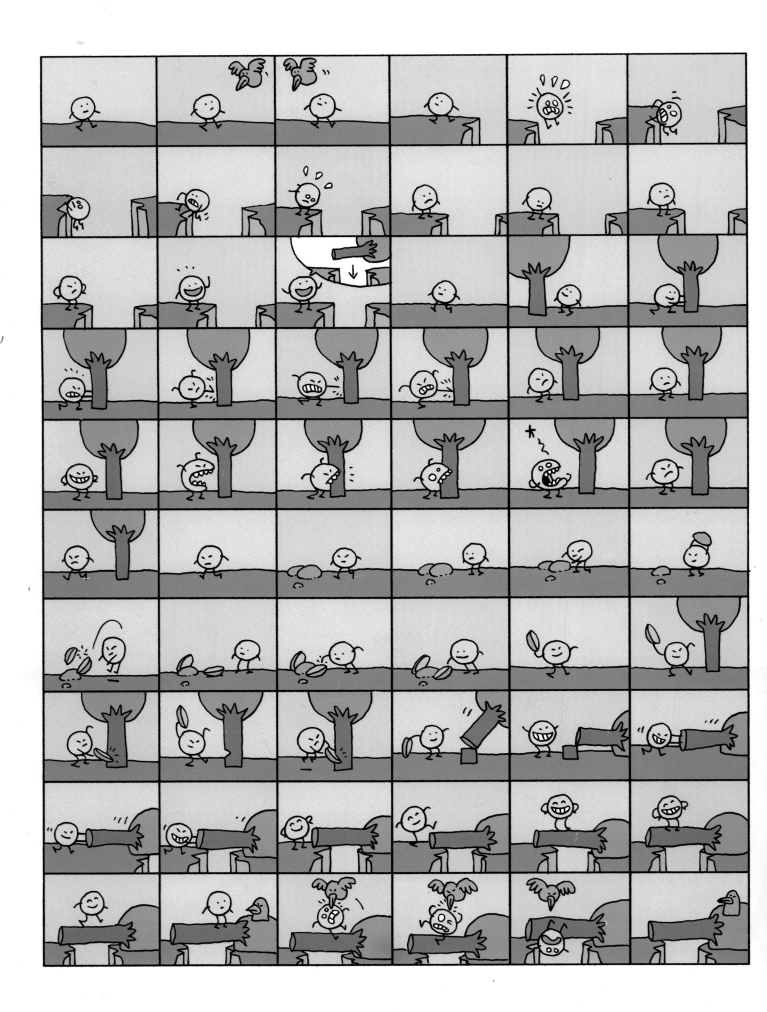

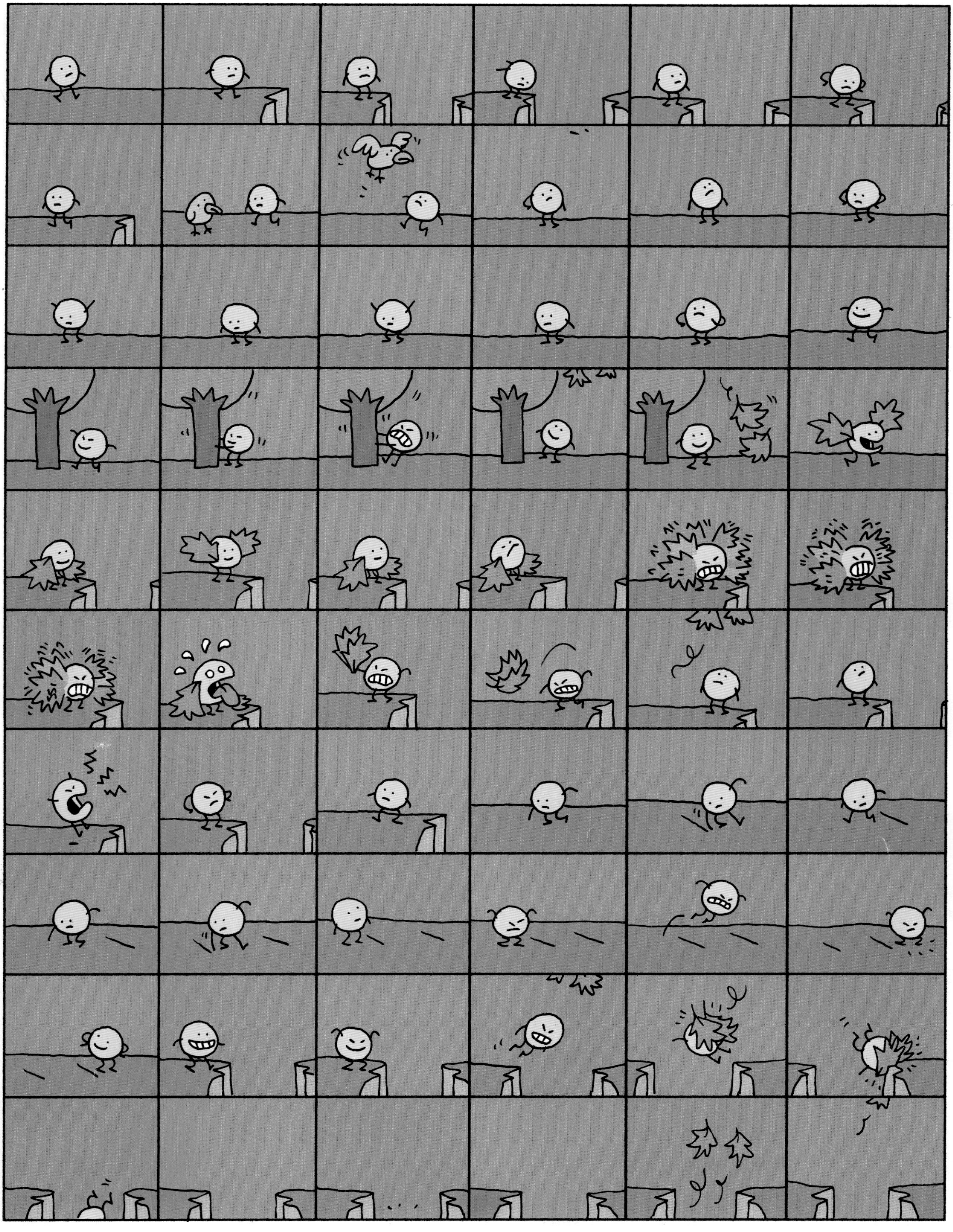

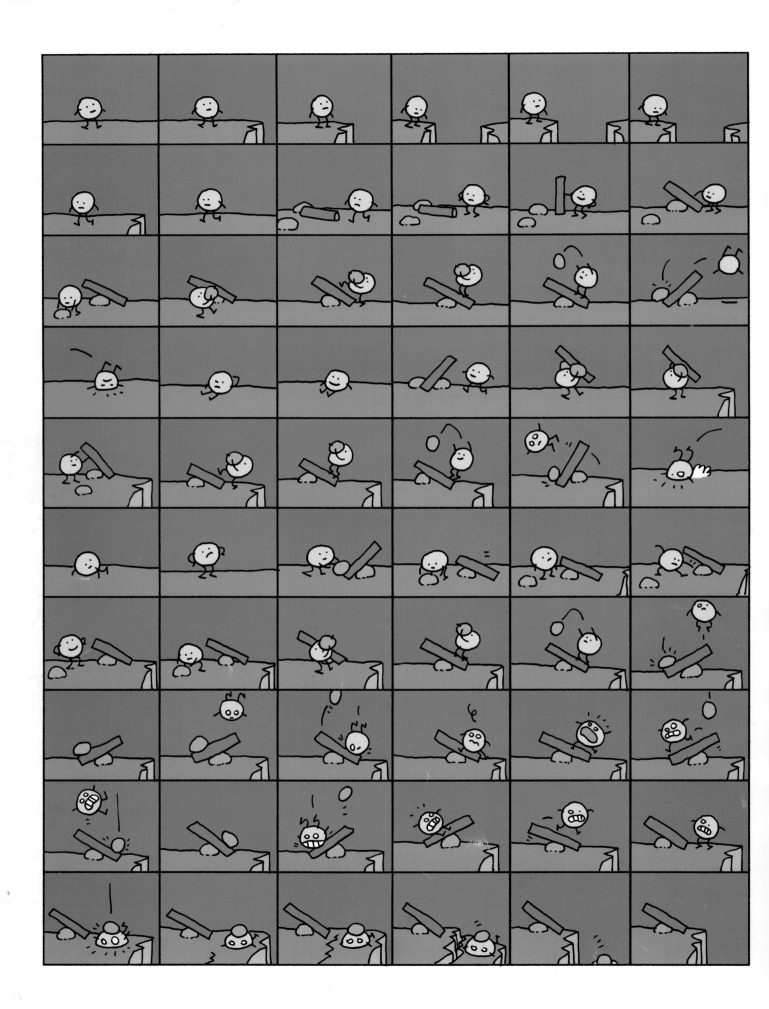

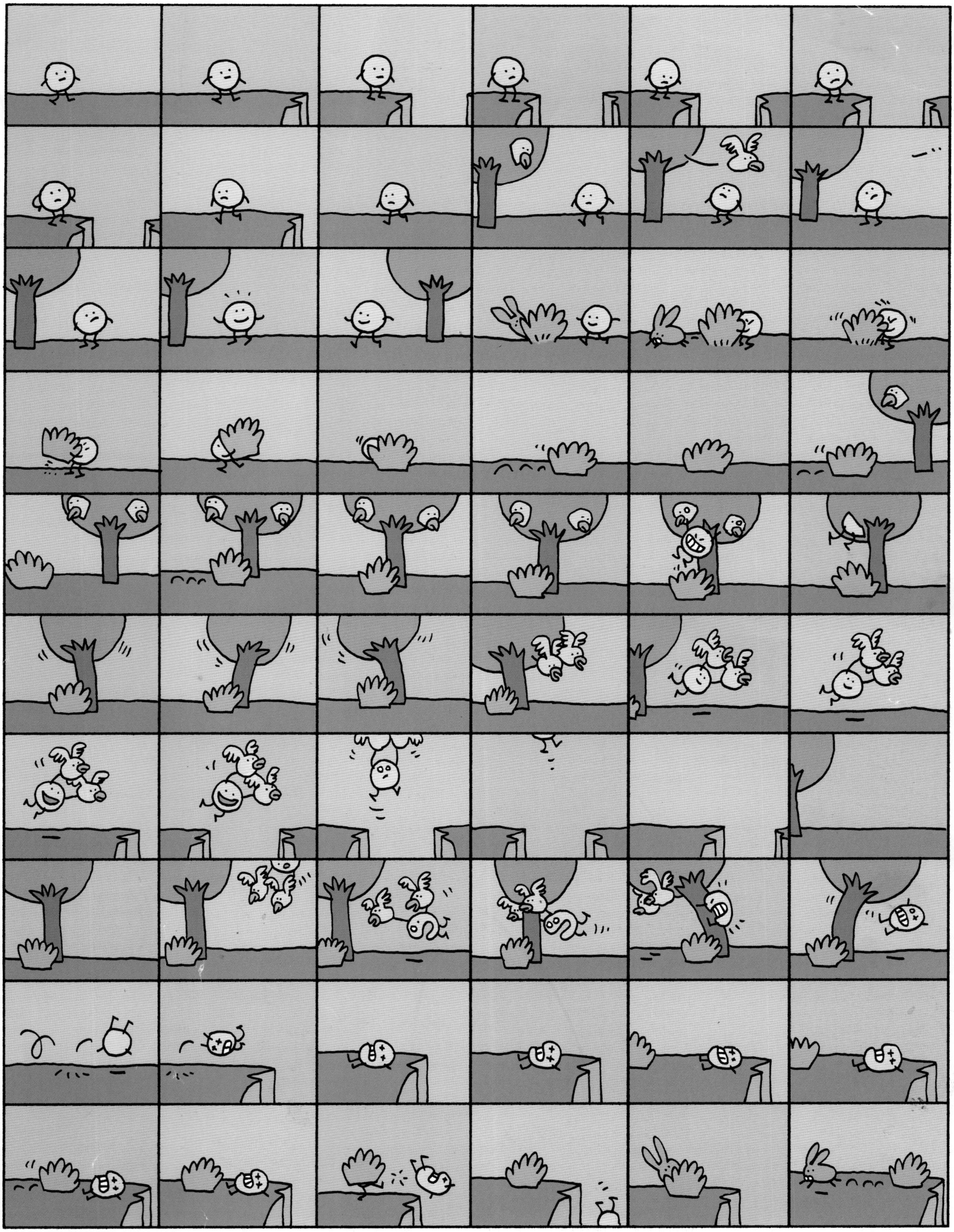

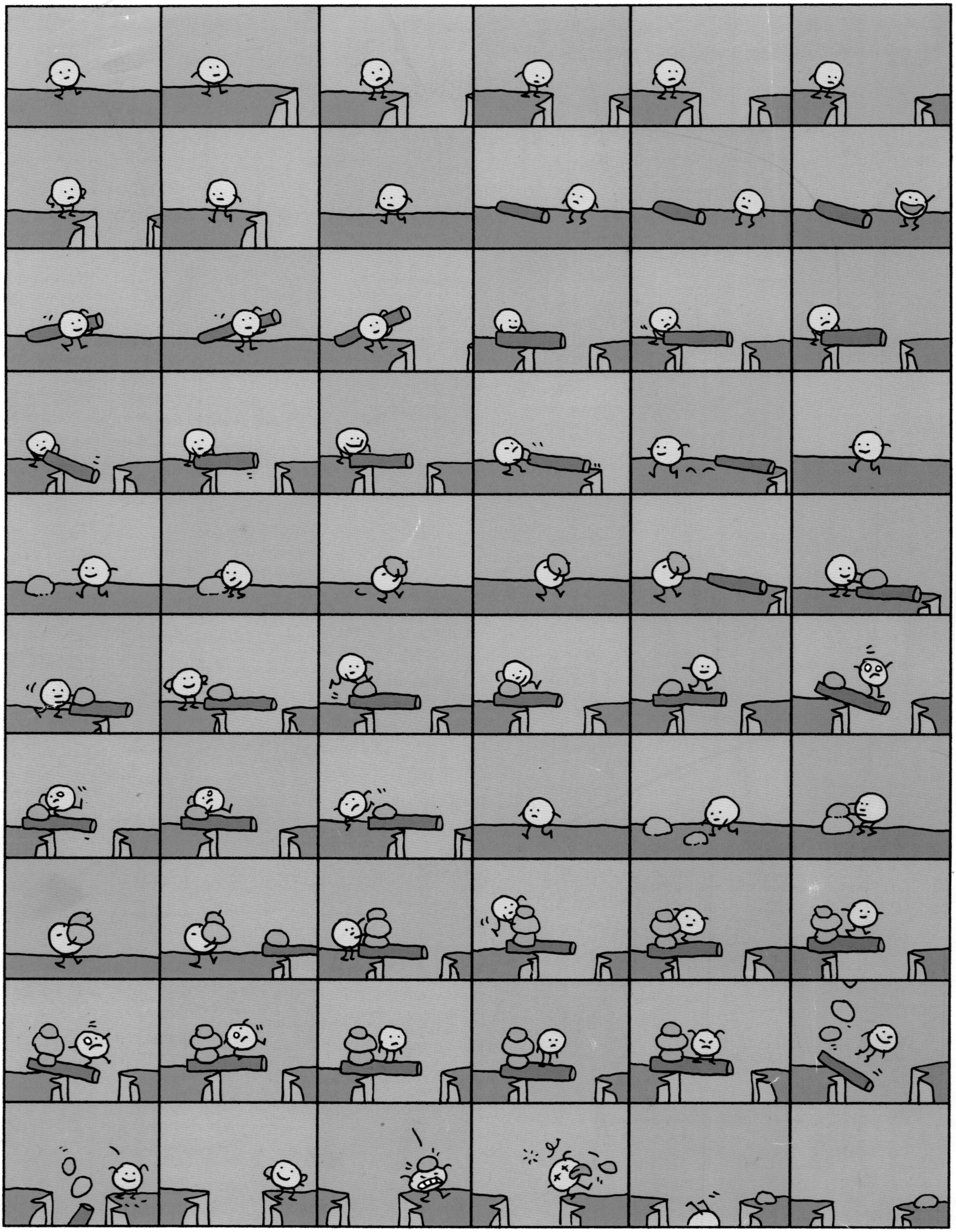

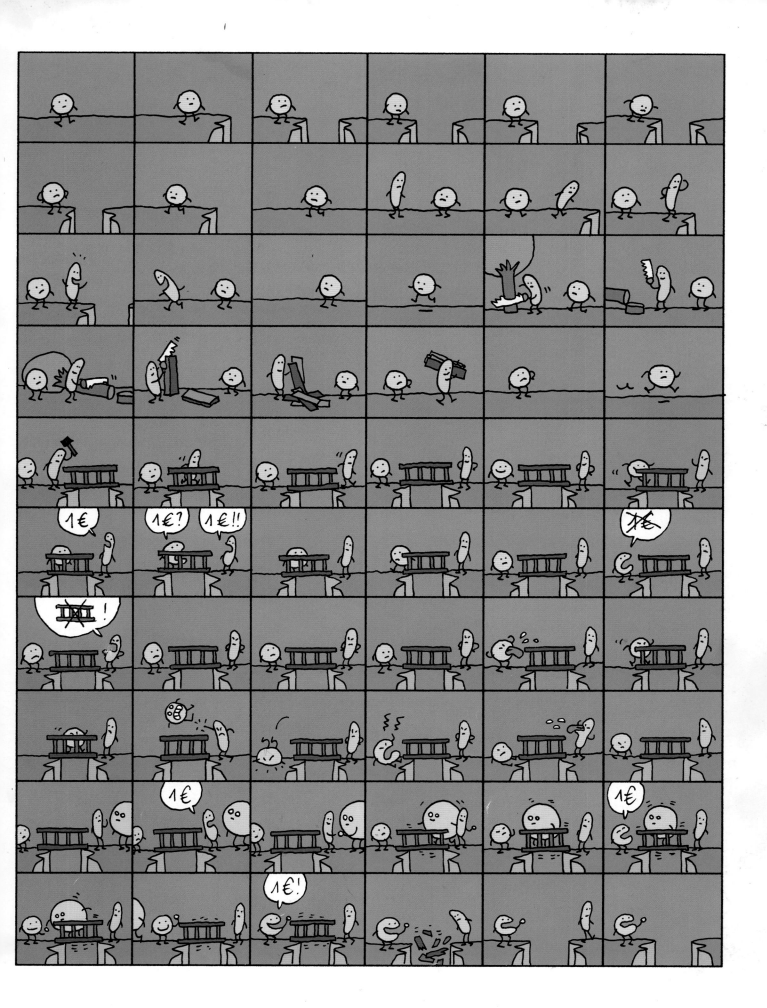

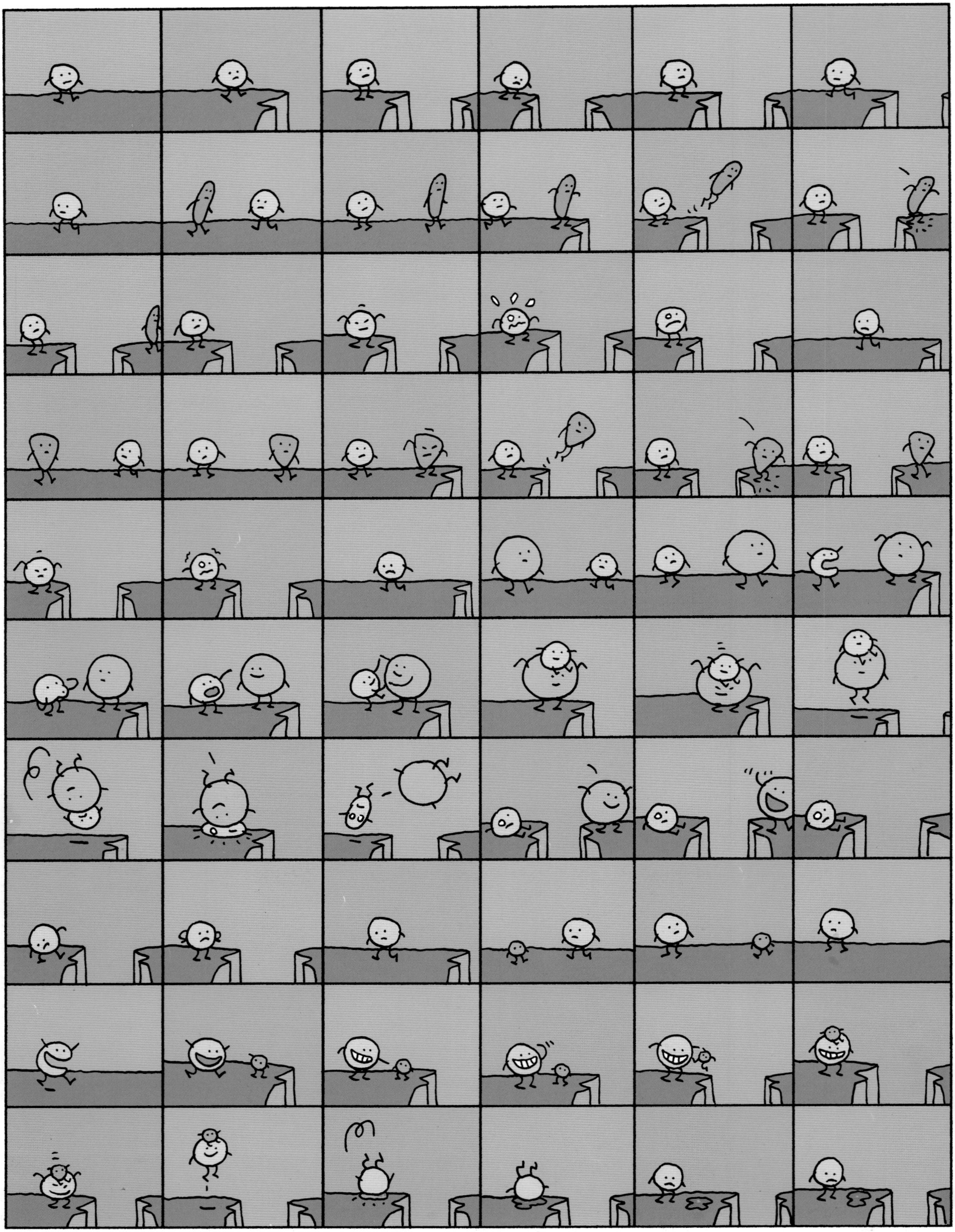

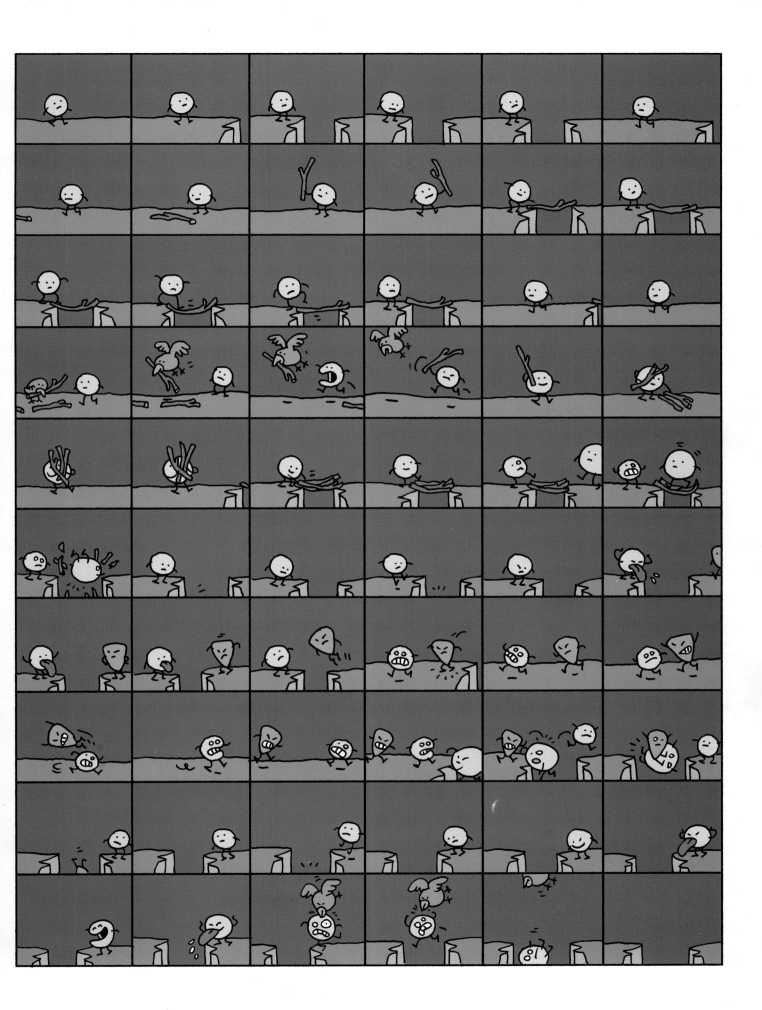

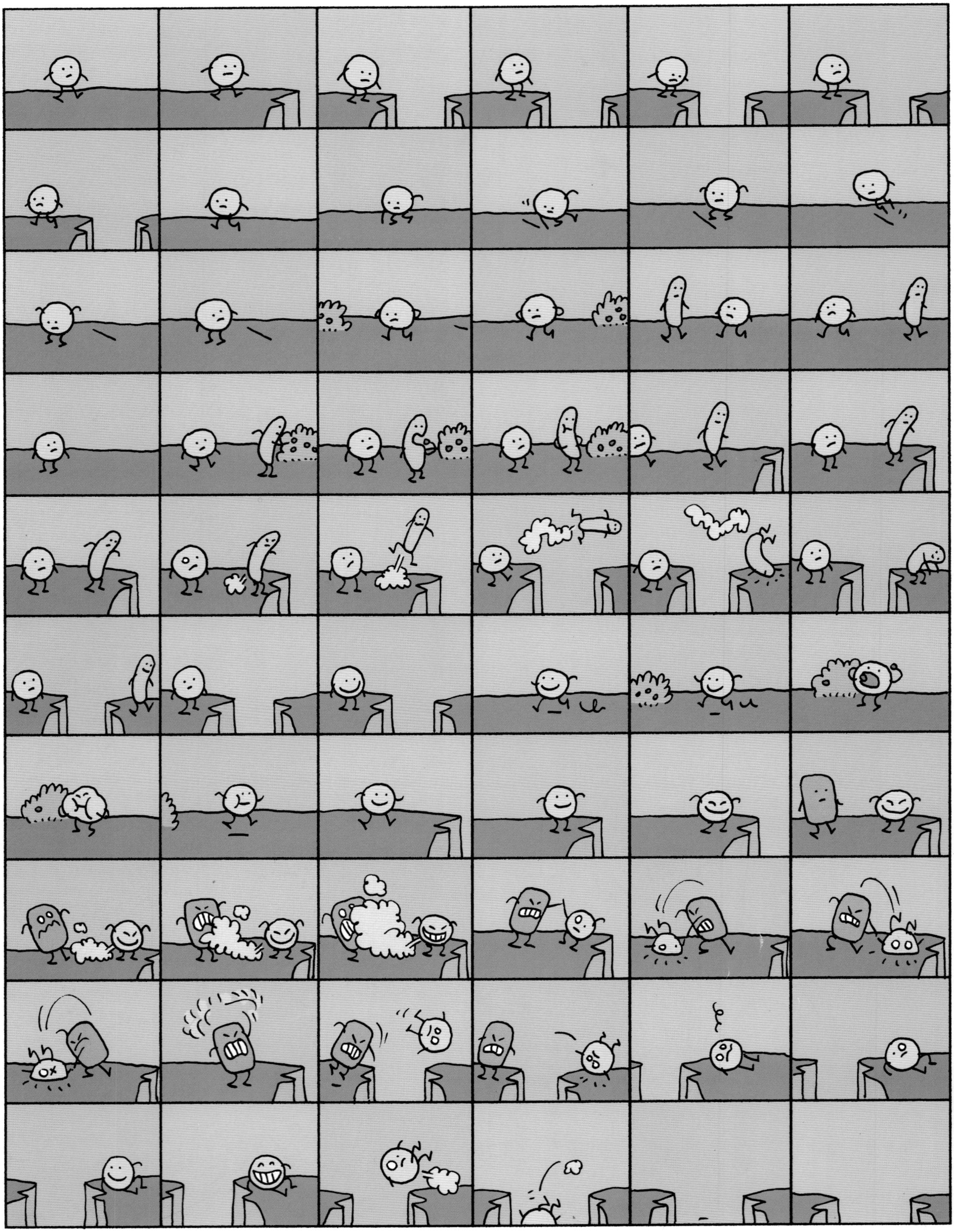

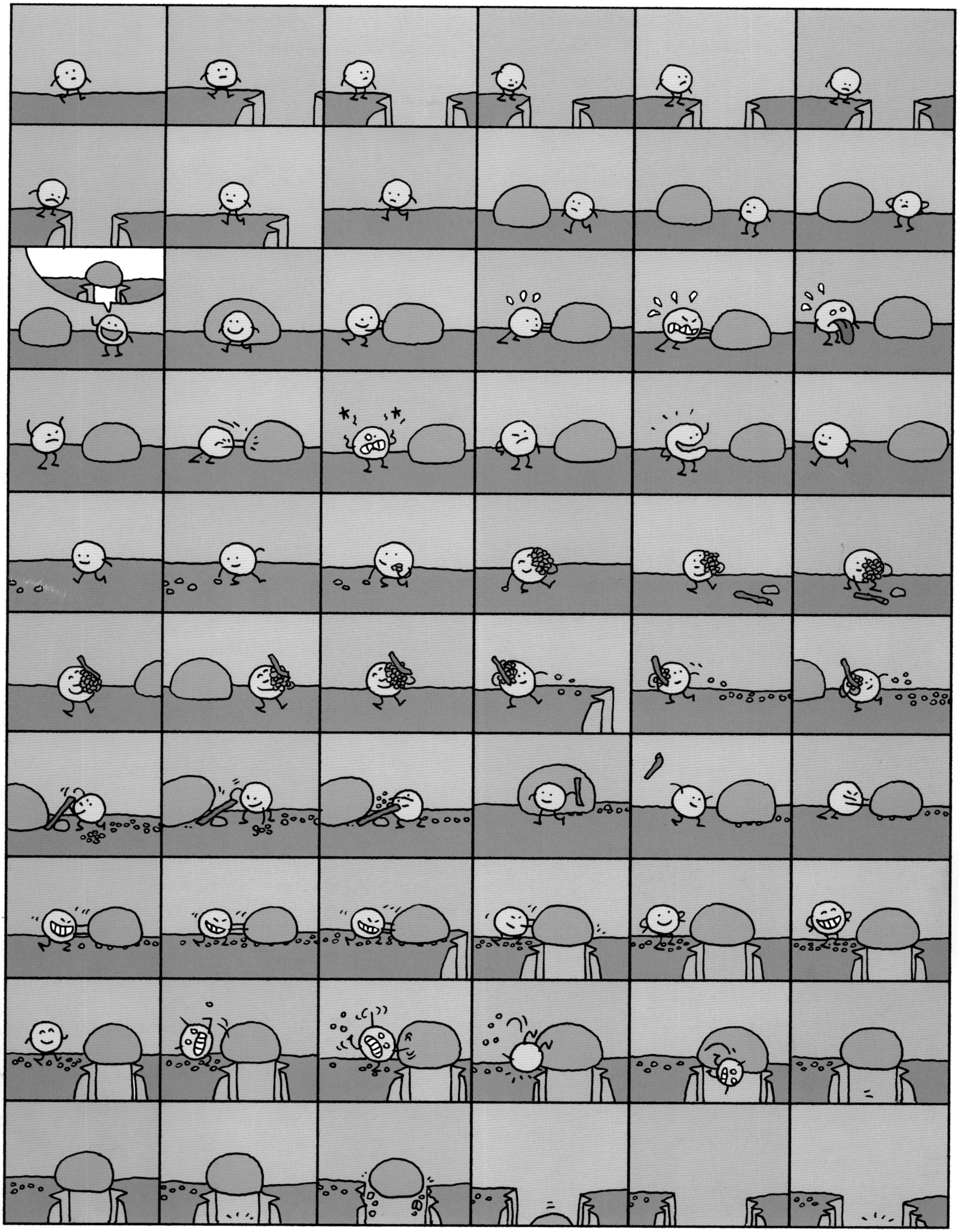

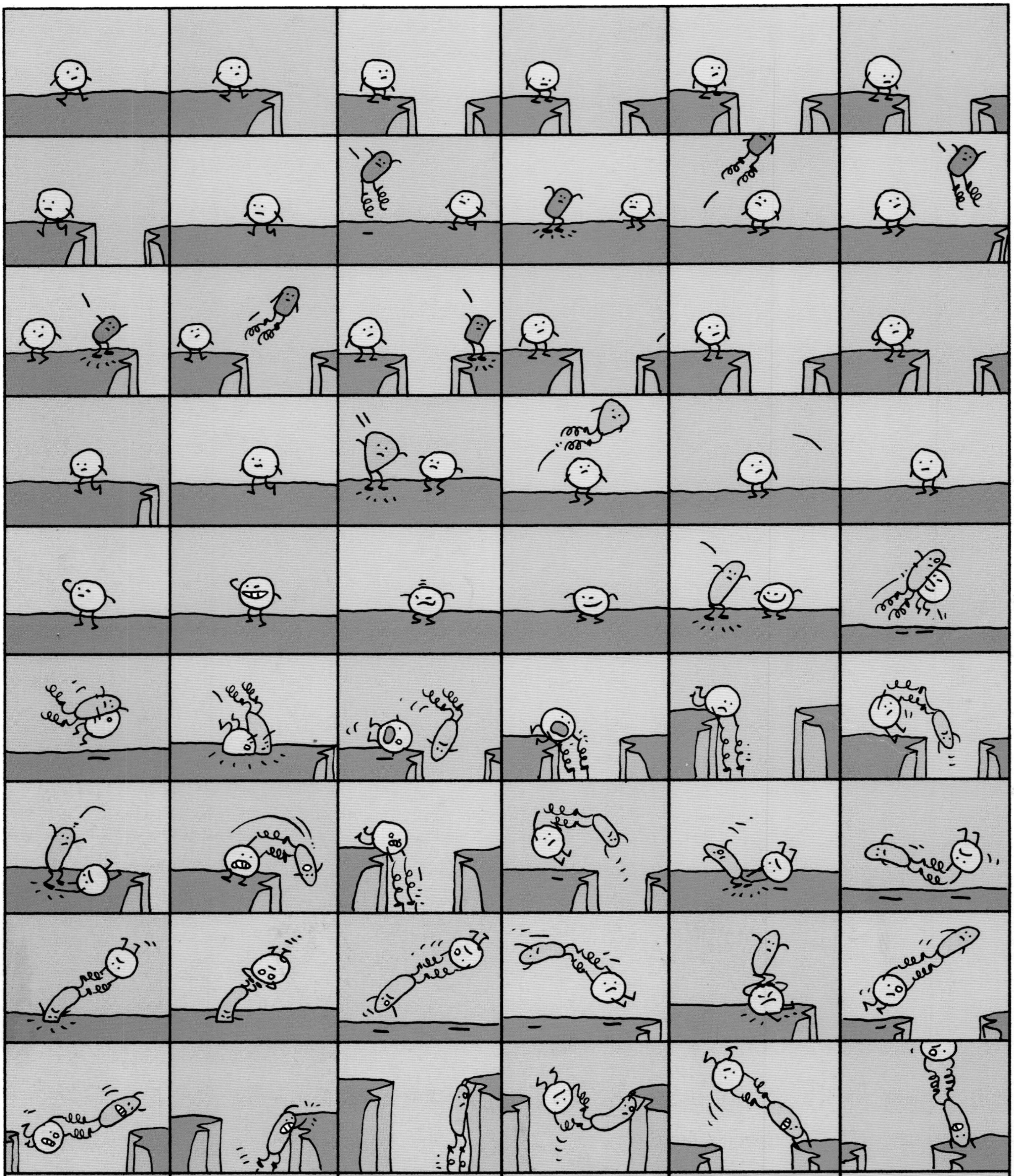

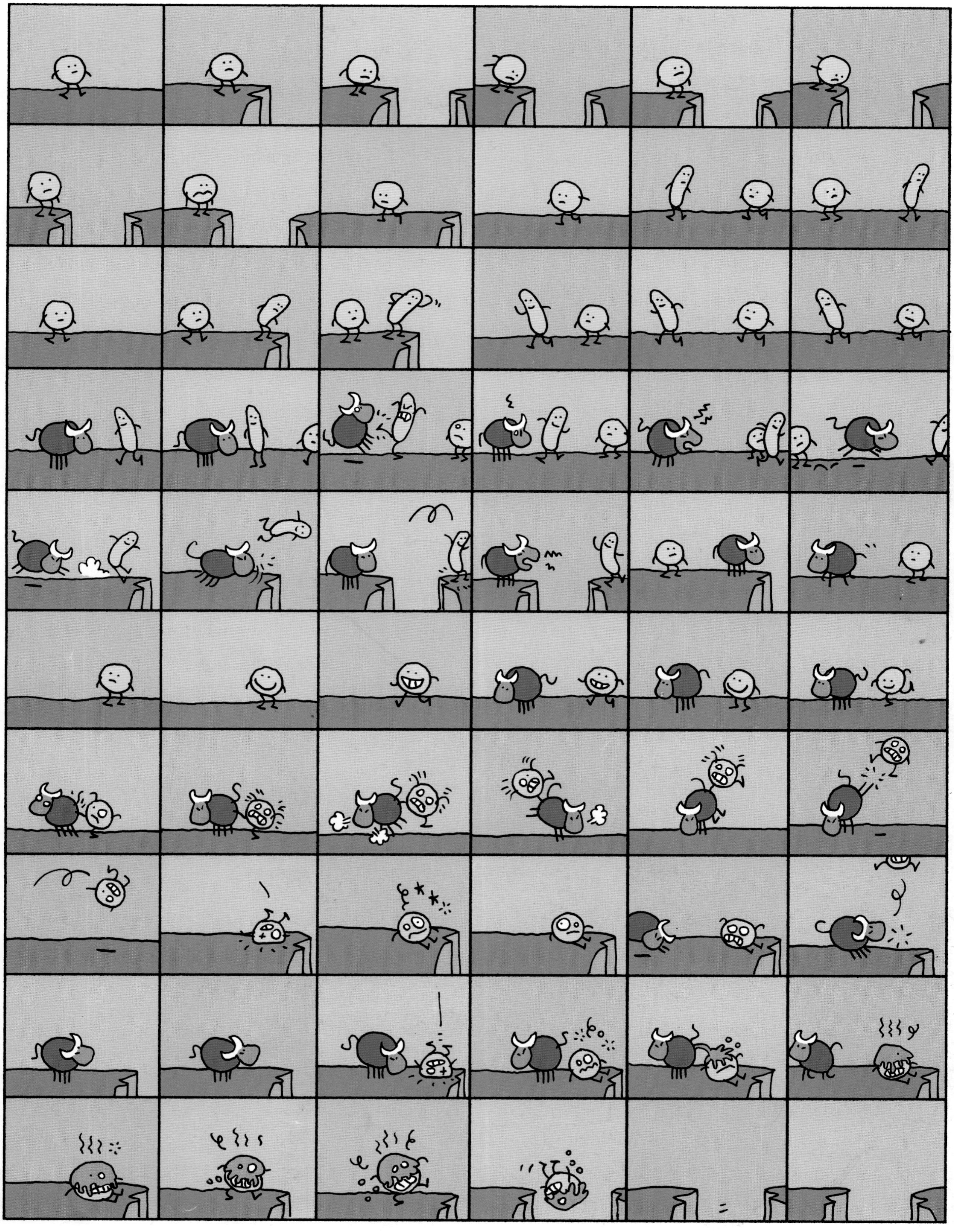

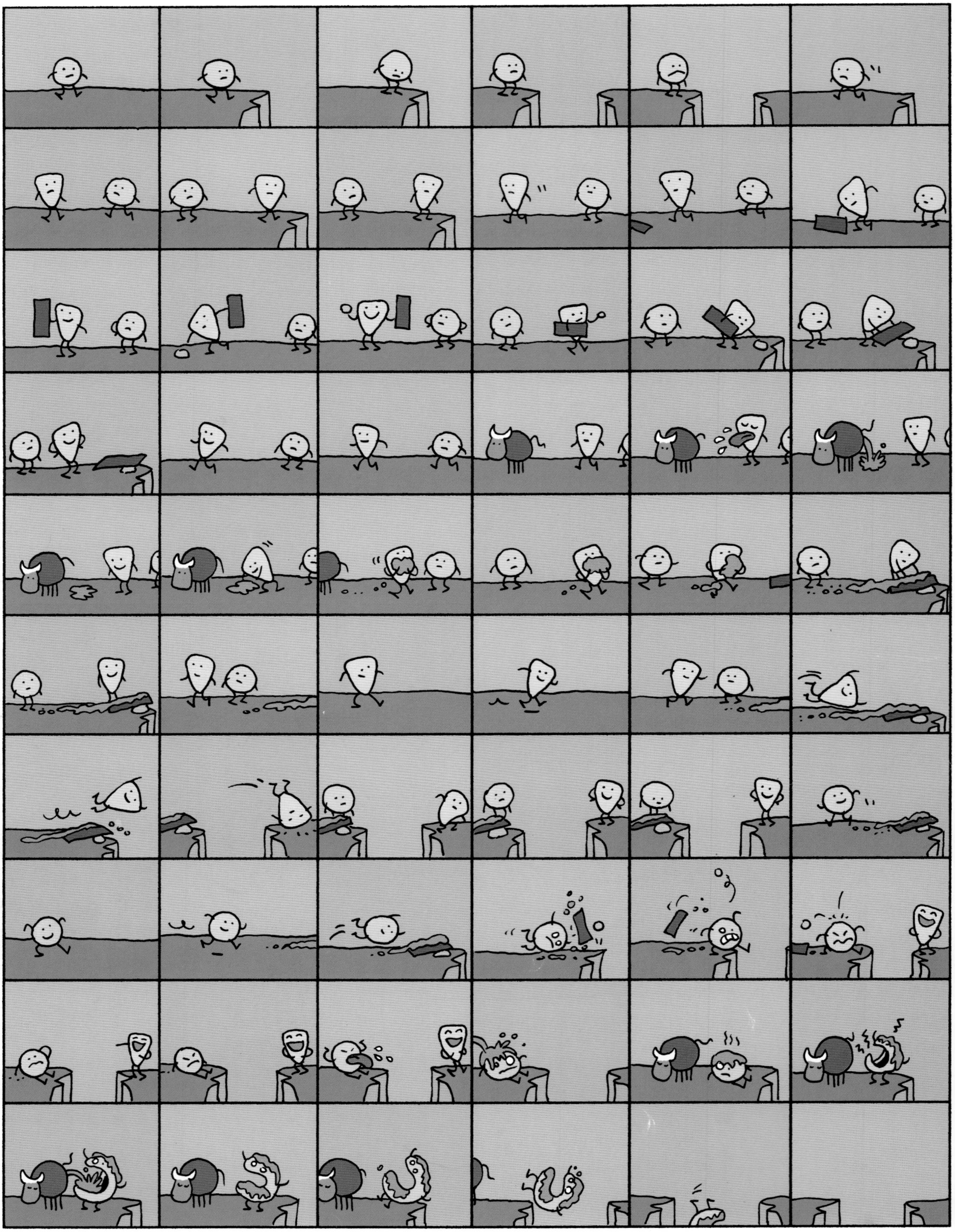

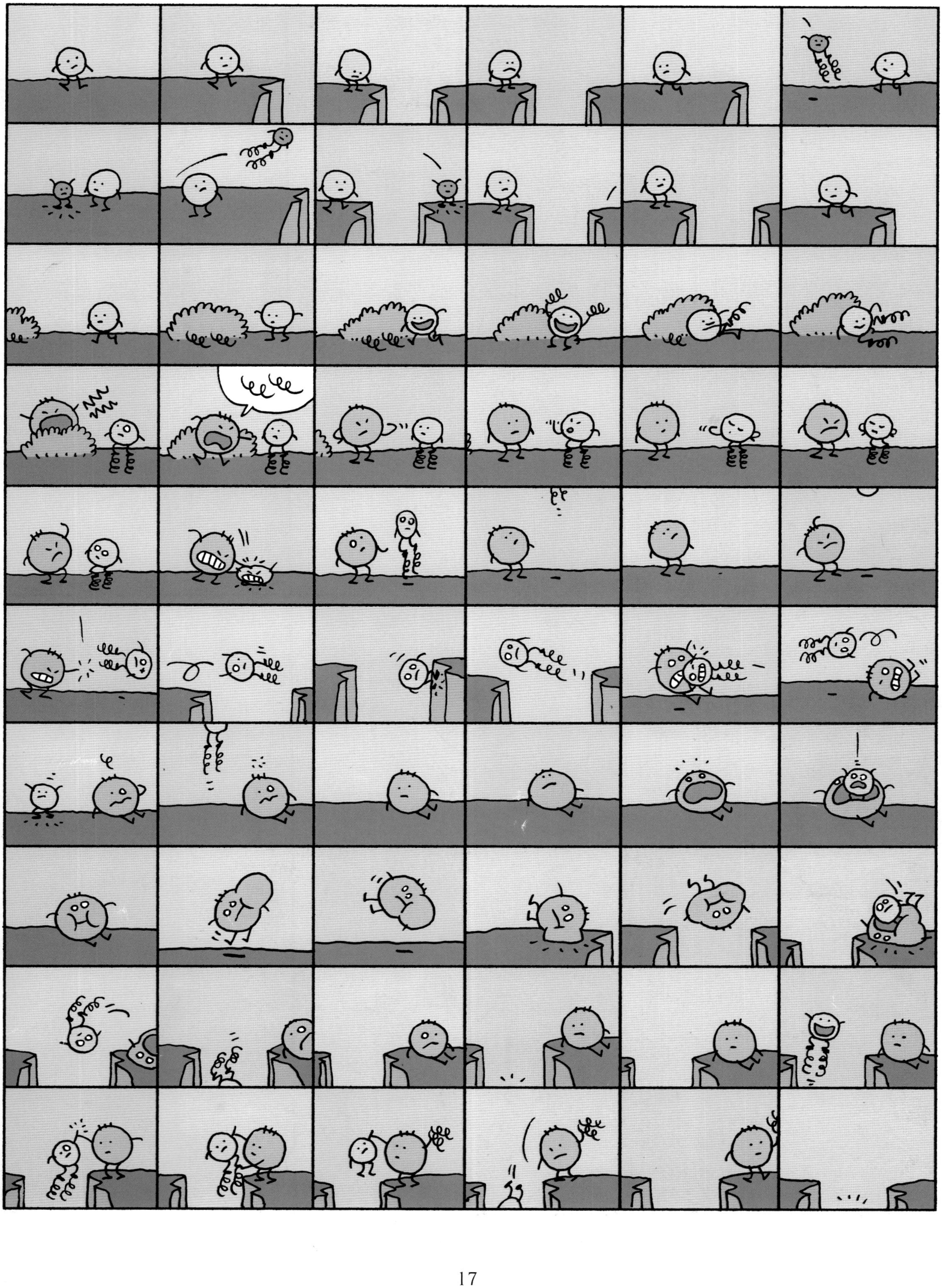

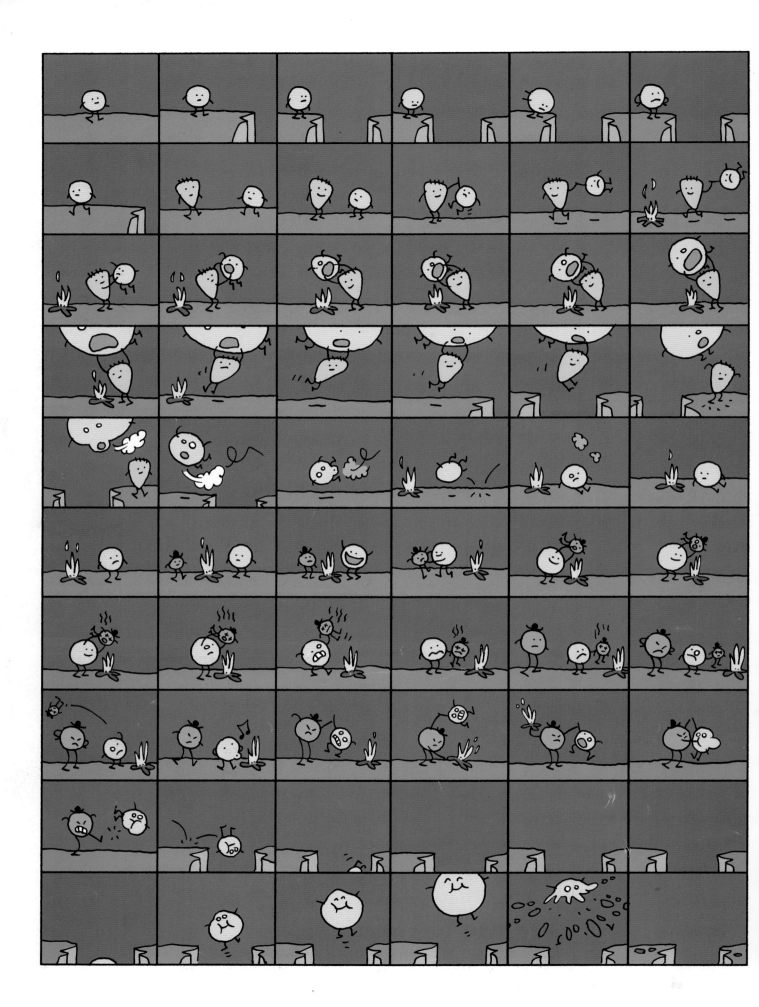

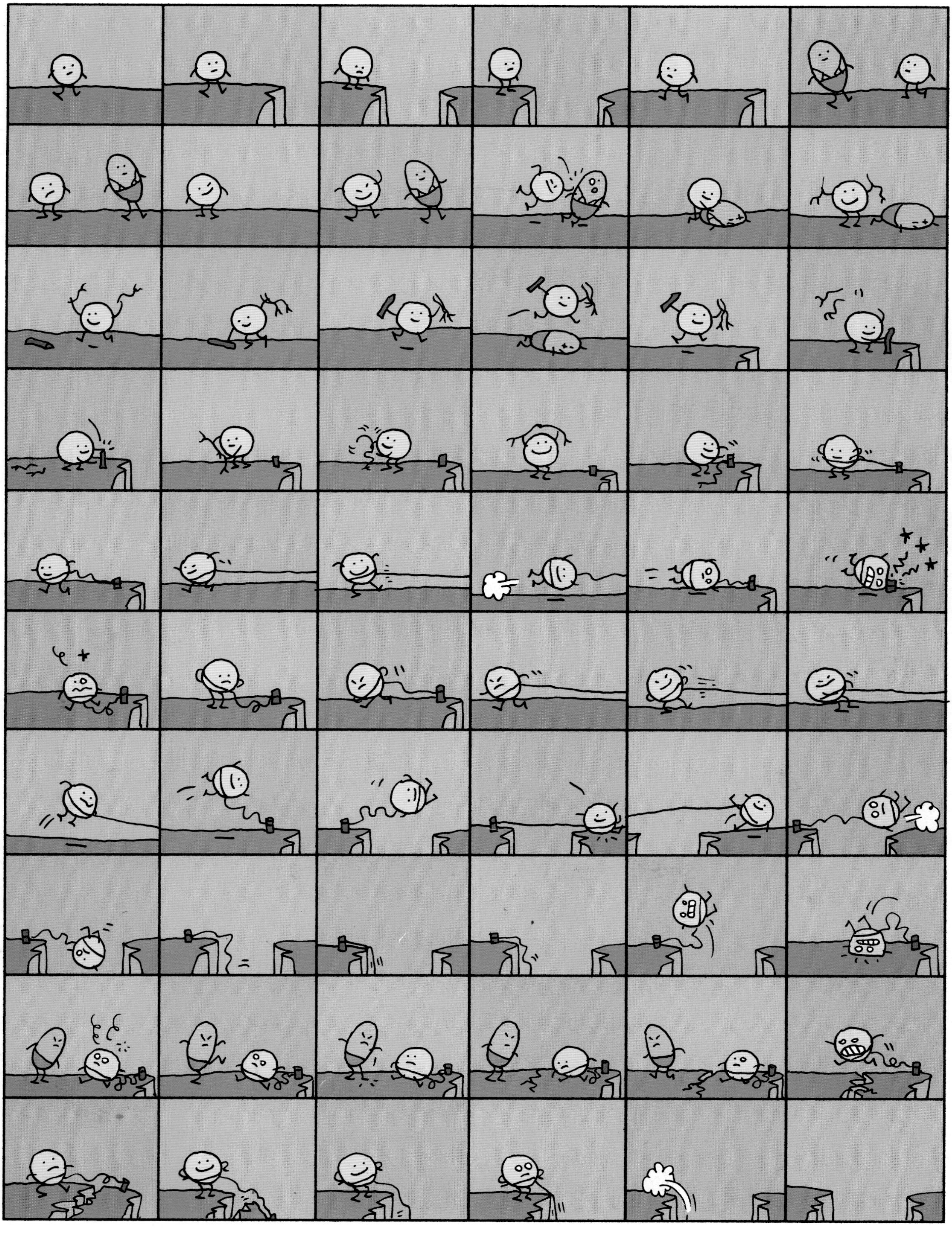

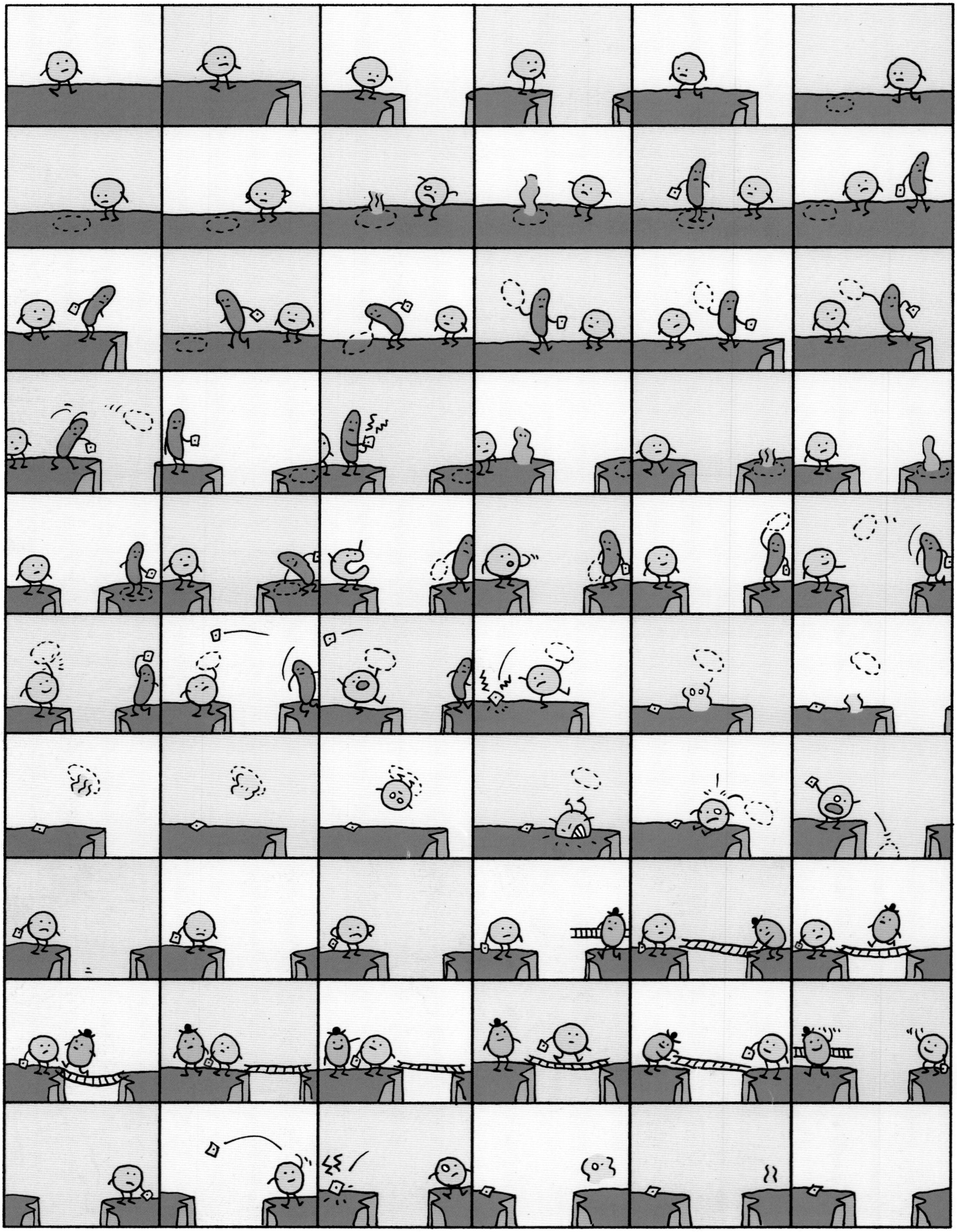

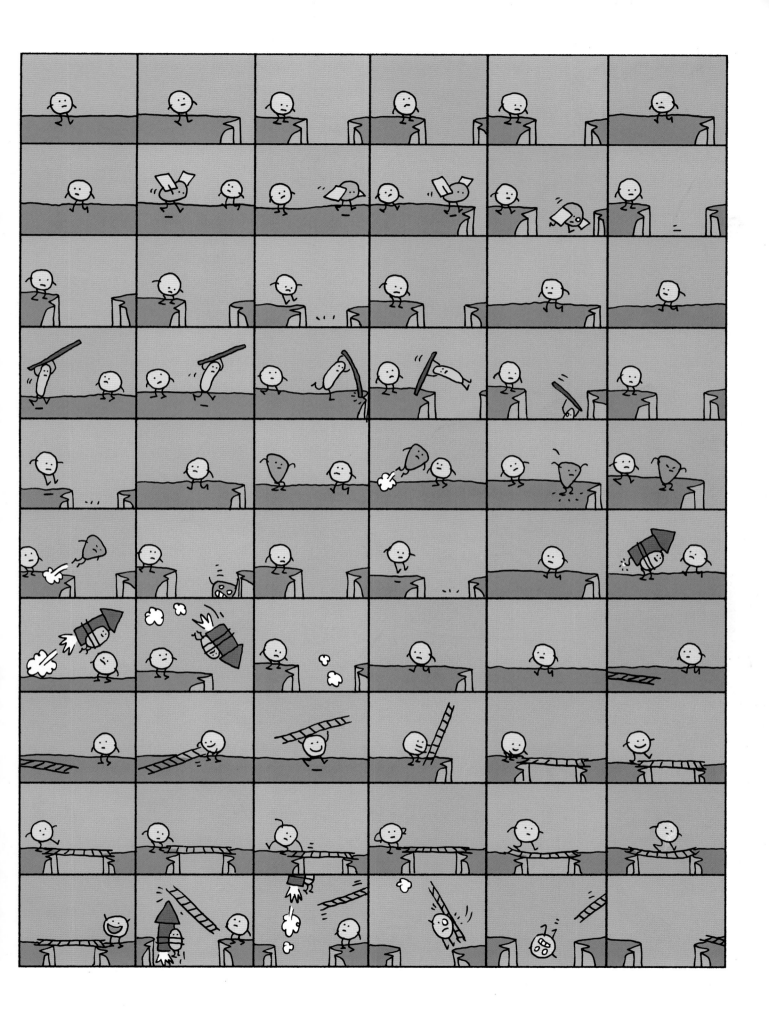

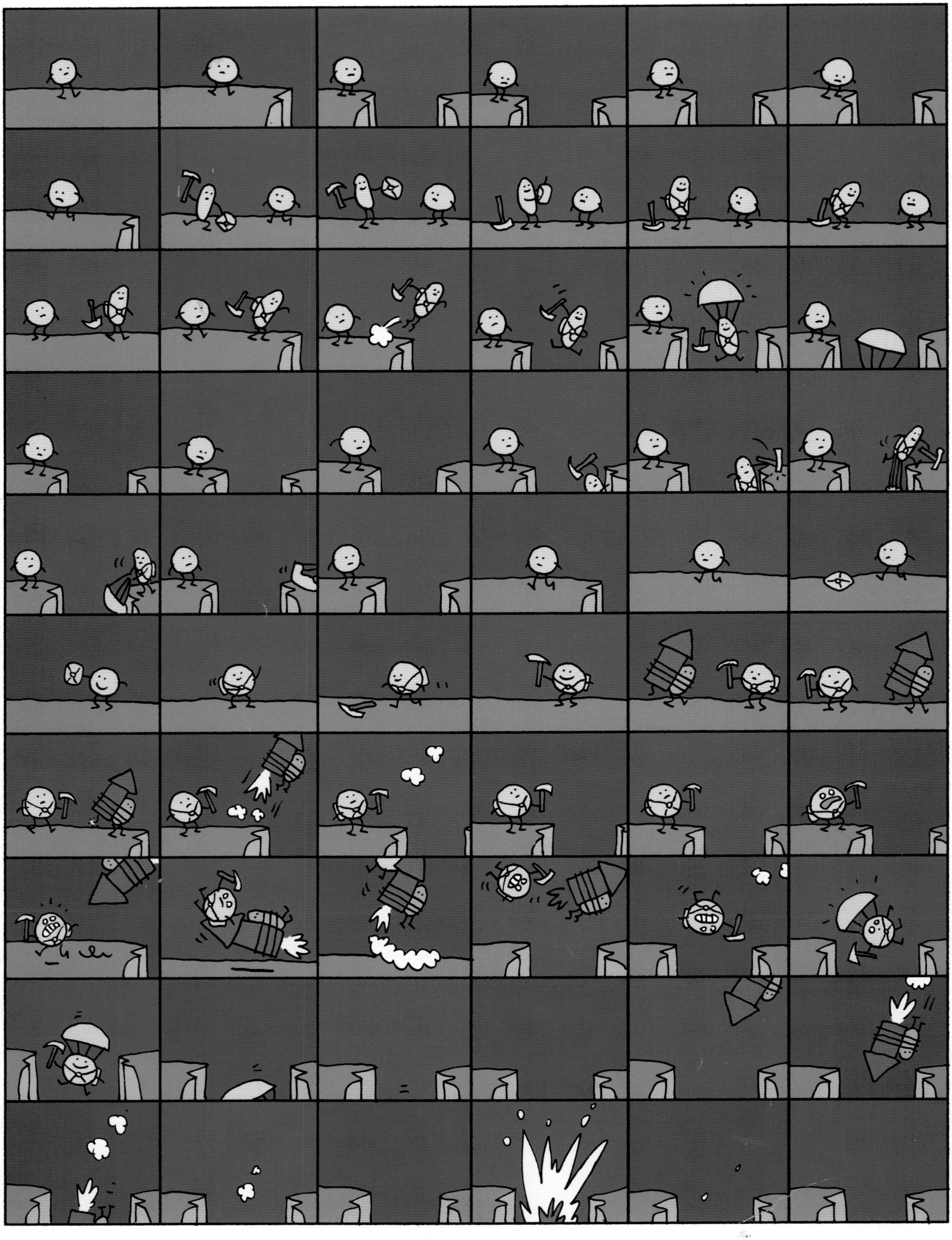

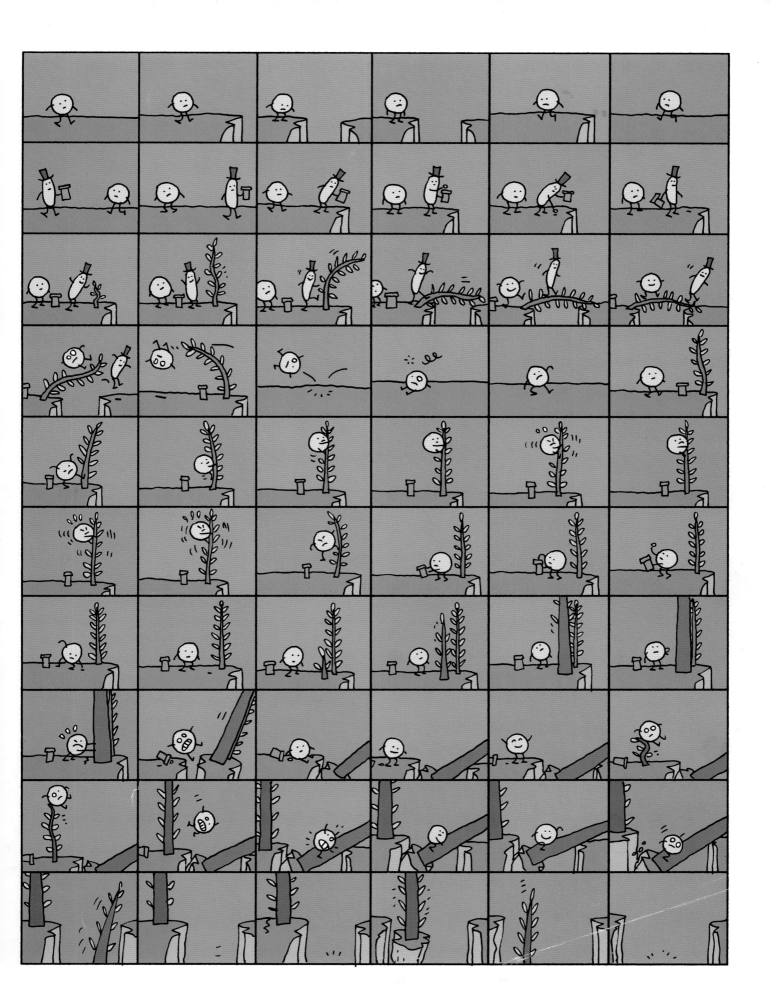

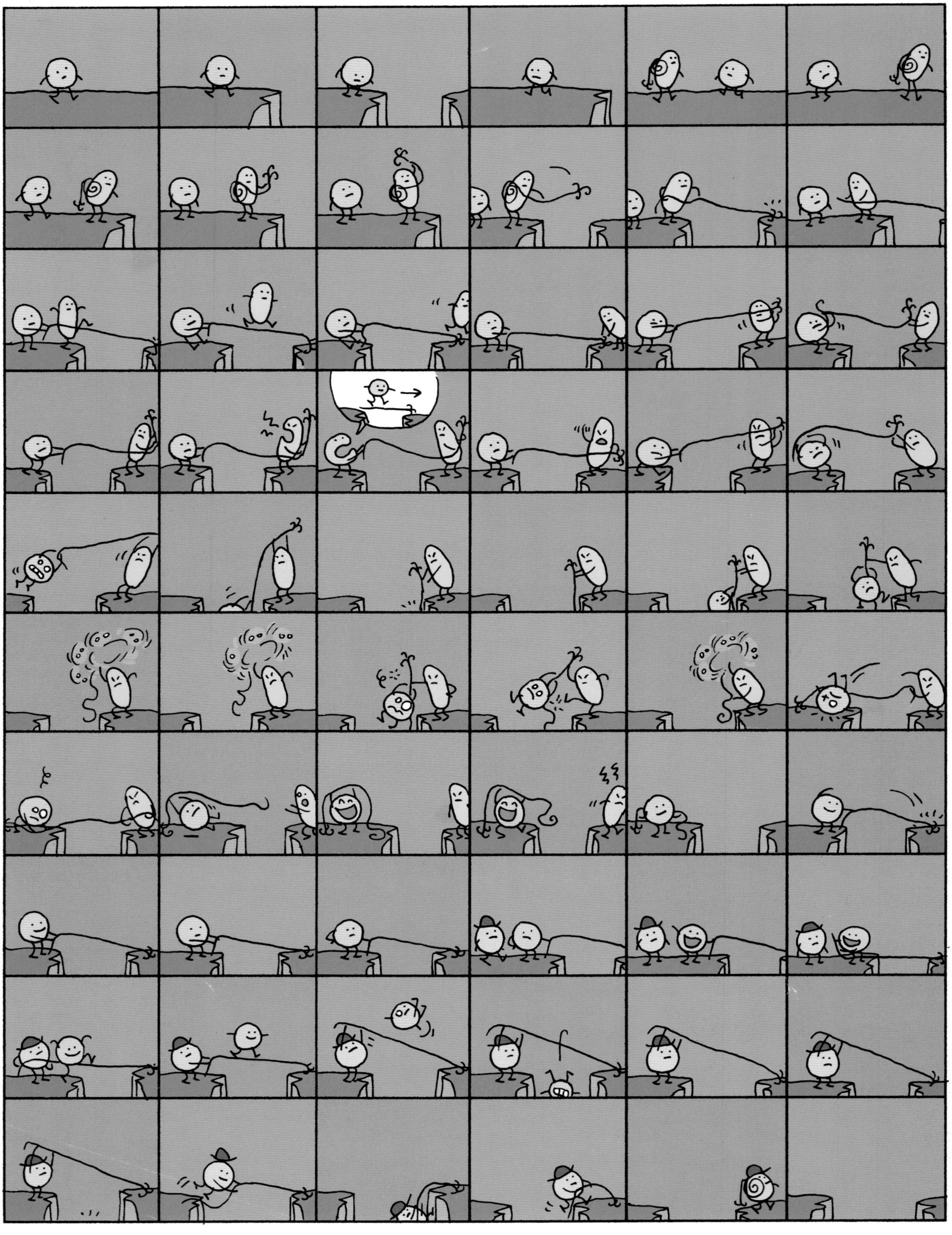

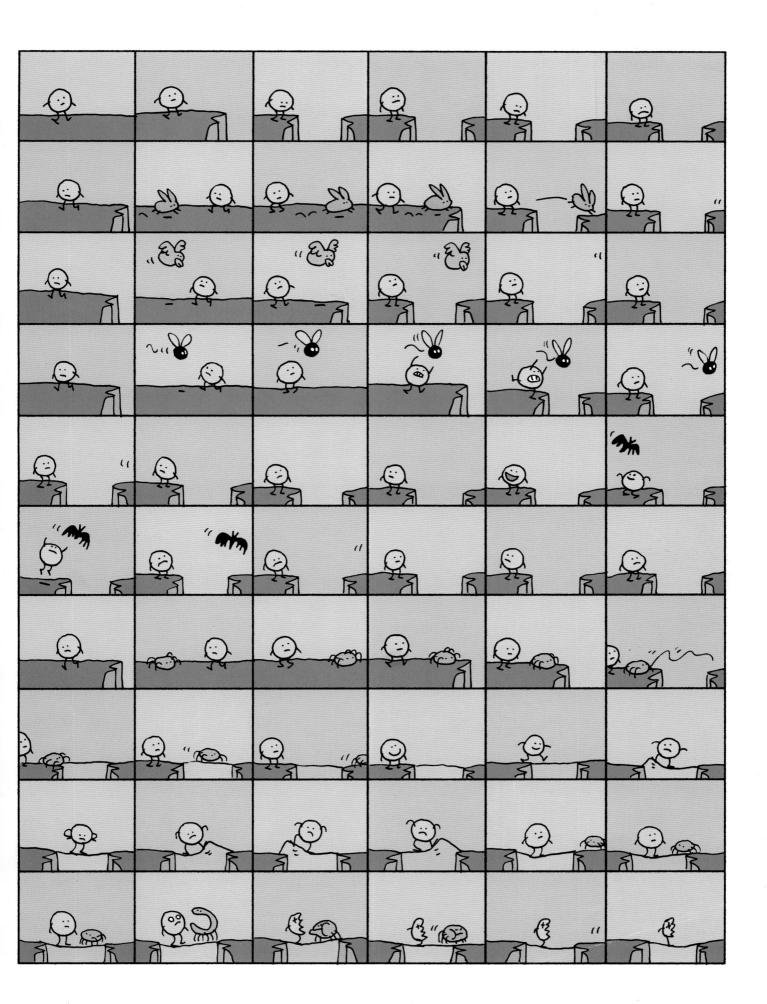

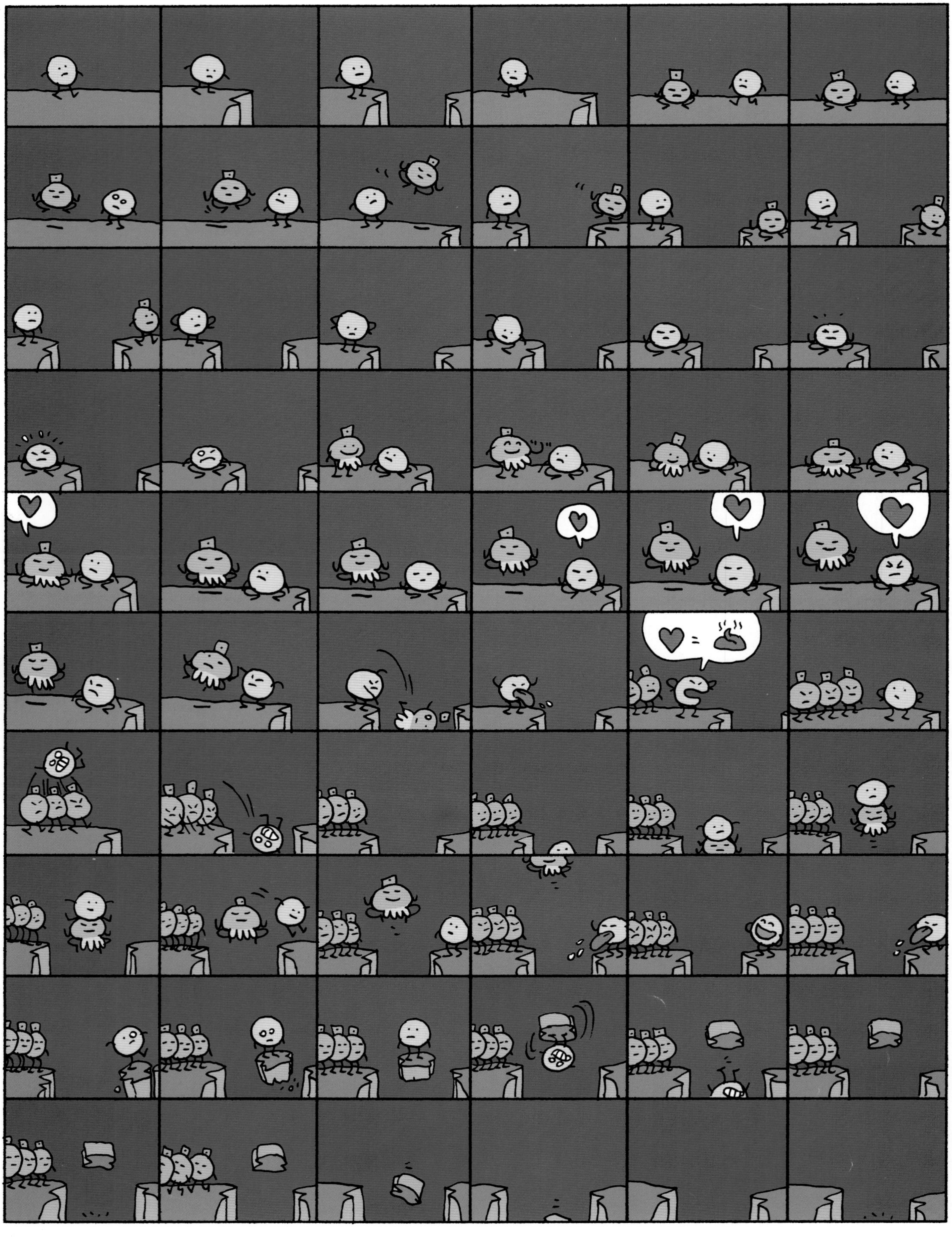

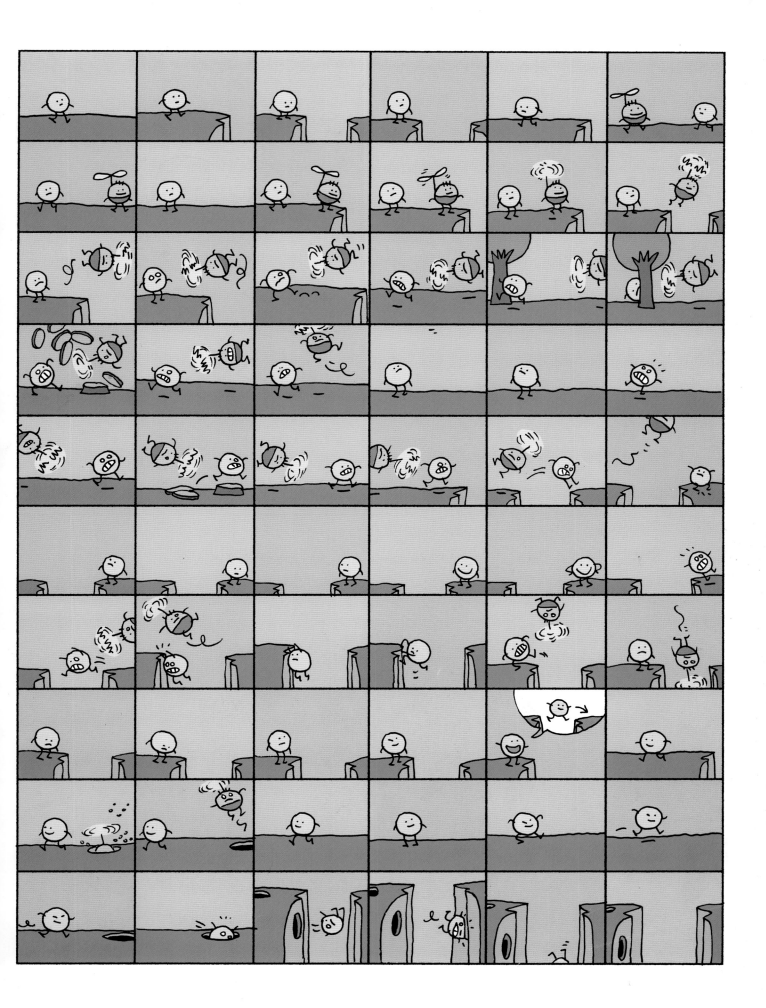

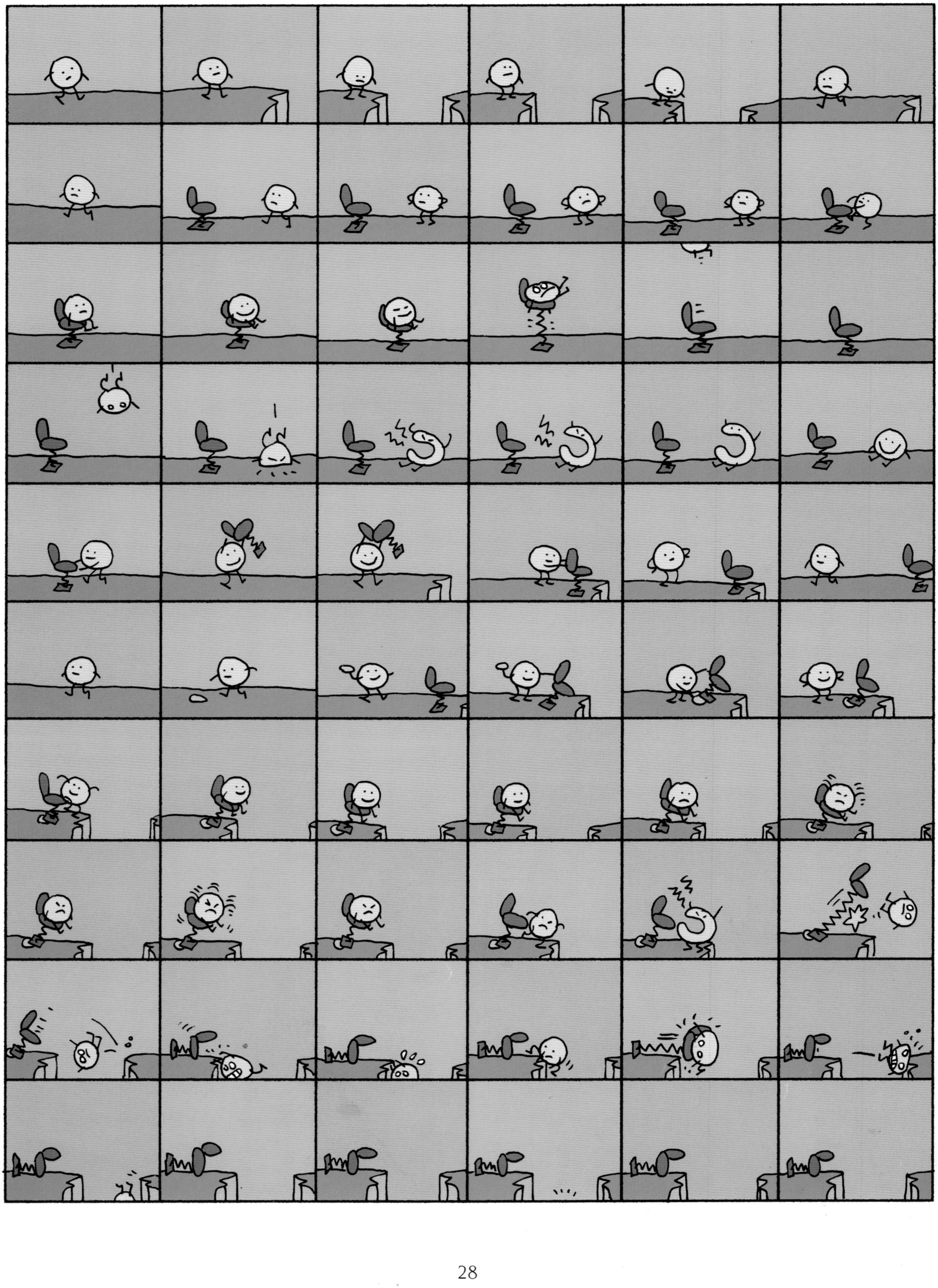

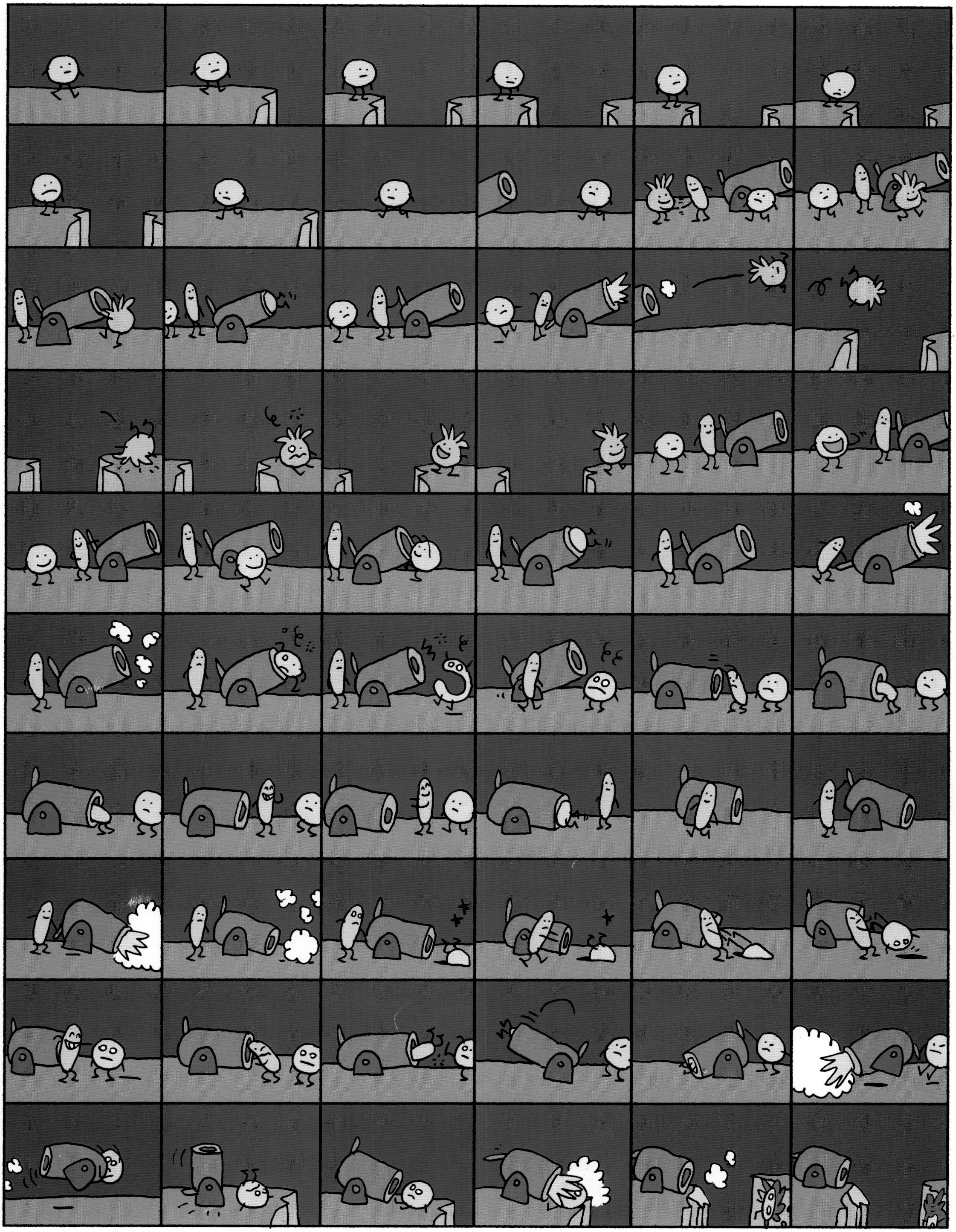

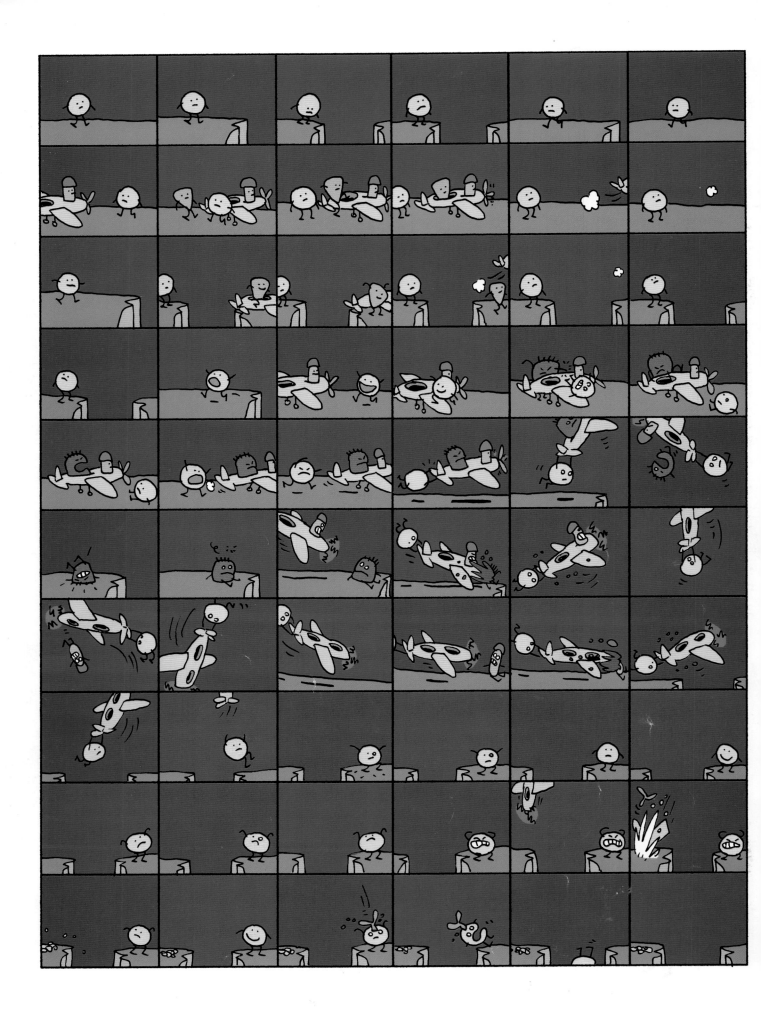

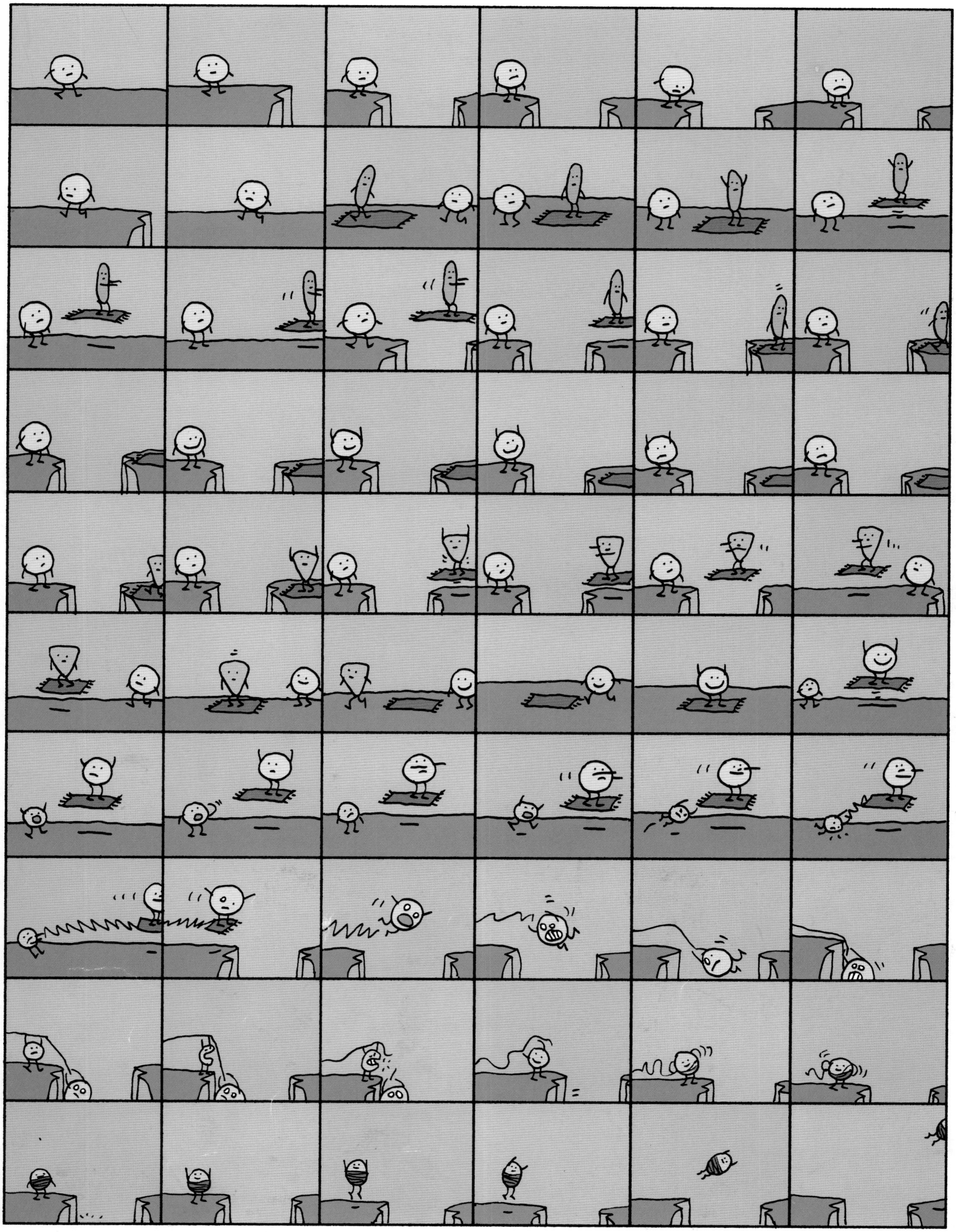

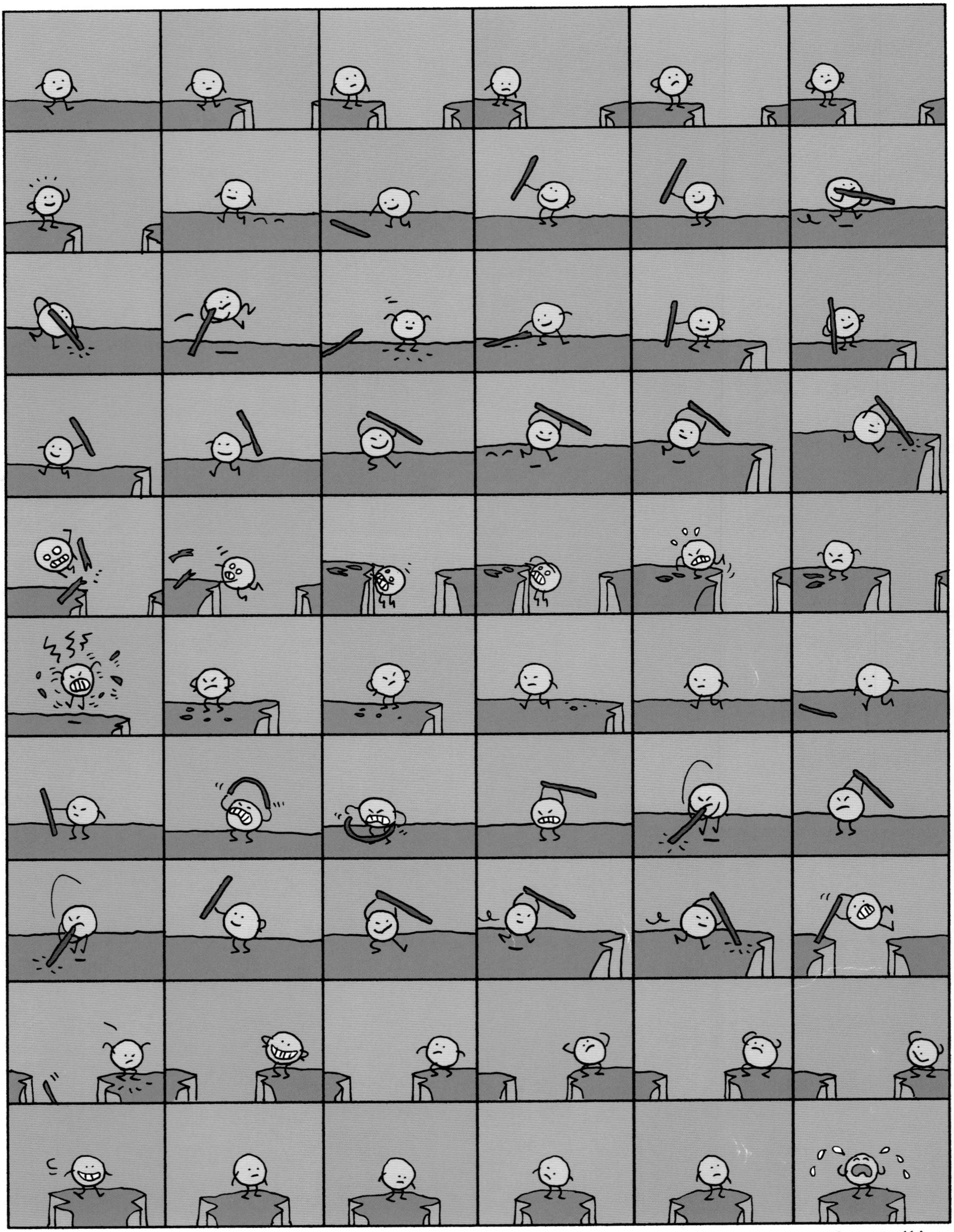

LEWIS TRONDHEIM